PAPER AIRPLANE

PAPER
AIRPLANE

ALLAN KAPLAN

1817

HARPER & ROW, PUBLISHERS
New York, Evanston, San Francisco, London

The following poems first appeared in the magazines listed below:

The Nation: "*New York Times* Weather Map," "Tonight," "Ave Maria"
Chelsea Review: "As If," "To the Poet on His 35th Birthday"
Poetry: "Poem" (I don't know whether I'm light or heavy)
Art and Literature: "The Usher," Wives," "Poem (Down the stoop, 2 screaming boys . . .)"
New American Review: "Lilar, 1968," "Homage to Andrew Marvell"
Quarterly Review of Literature: "My Strangeness," "Marvelous," "Hudson Street," "The Heart," "Through New Jersey Via the Greyhound"
Extensions: "Poem (How many hours am/I a presence)"
Poems Now: "Big Party"
Paris Review: "July Poem"
Iowa Review: "Love Poem"
"Thinking of Frank" appeared in a novel, *Seven Years of Winter,* by Erje Ayden, published by London Magazine.

FIRST EDITION

STANDARD BOOK NUMBER: 06-012254-4

LIBRARY OF CONGRESS CATALOG CARD NUMBER: 76-138741

CONTENTS

ONE / AS IF

TWO / SOUTH AMERICAN MUSIC

THREE / WATCHING PORNOGRAPHIC FILMS

FOUR / AVE MARIA

PART ONE

AS IF

THROUGH NEW JERSEY, VIA THE GREYHOUND

The pretty shingles of New Jersey fly by in millions.
Telephone wires go like Earth's endlessness over the Queen Anne's
    lace,
and towns grow taller trees that beg to be recalled
                        as they slip through my fingers.

Browsing in *Selected Coleridge* to
"—only the ideal is in good poetry, there are no accidents—"
Oh, Samuel, you aren't being truthful here
in this state of muddy creeks and piles of old tires and smoke!
Meanwhile, wide patches of burnt-out grass coming again and again
                      recapture the hours of my excesses.
And the cord of white roadline draws our bus up, as if it were a flag,
                up swiftly
nearer the border
                past which my life will soar
to where there are morning glories and a diner
            that's open all night long,
                  that belongs to Pete and Betsy!

TRAFFIC

How pleasant to walk the streets.
The warmth of a hand has been lingering on my side,
while cars disappear and come, honking occasionally, as a thought
                                going through my brain.
How is it I do not love the girl who stayed with me
and touched my side while she slept last night?
Honk, honk! Another thought. Honk!
A star falls, like the hand of the calm sleeper, making a gentle arc
                                in the night.

See, two teen-agers walking wearing vinyl skirts, so short and yellow.
O like enthusiasm their hair falls abundantly. Look,
their knees are naked savages.
I remember Michael, my friend, saying whatever brings you into
      the New
                                is a positive good. Forward!
My spirit rises out of myself to be greeted in midair by loveliness
                                of the girls.
My love turns spiritual in midair!
On my side the warmth of the hand lingers, like the star my
astrologer saw bringing to me luck and a joy to be with others,
                                as it crosses the sky.
How marvelous that short skirts bring youthful knees into our city.
How marvelous is Michael's idea that shapes today for me.
O my own body, and Michael, all my friends,
the traffic where cars may gently bump like curious strangers
                                who are open-hearted,
and the thoroughfare of my head with its traffic passing,
      and the light of this hour
                                are OMNIPRESENCE

LILAR, 1968

The wallpaper in this motel displays strings of individual roses
browned by the saltiness of the Atlantic seacoast.
As now,
roses have flown like escaped balloons into my view:

Once
staring—striking out of a wave, a freestyle,
forearm a tattoo.
This flower
moved over the sea like a miracle up down
when I was seven or eight, awing me; and
when an oil landscape of sheep on a dark hillside, many years later,
made a sober
mood more sober
than it ought to be,
I turned and the pink roses reappeared across the bedspread—

but their reappearance only disturbs the surface like the
"How awful"
one cries at dying reappearing in the newspaper
as in today's:
Miss Lilar Kestler, after chaining a fox terrier
to a railing,
was shot in the throat by a sniper
in Central Park
today
let's see now
Miss Lilar
today

Lancaster (smalltown) Pennsylvania daughter of a doctor
by walking dogs in Central Park
earned her living
escaping perhaps thereby the buildings an education
jobbed her for.
I think
she wanted to be a citizen among greenery, frisky also, to be
simply
two-legged
the walking Lilar.
Lilar, around intelligent circles, you and I do distinguish ourselves
like a faint glow
around the moon.
I feel my arm yanked by five leashes!
I hear a faint barking.
What now?
"Bobby," I blurt, "Bobby Kennedy!" with not a word to say.
But I didn't think of
"Bobby" who passed before me on the exotic prosceniums
of public media.
The wallpaper's fake roses seem to have petals, Lilar,
that are real
as the virtue
of your existence,
which moistens my fingertips, smoothness in the press
of thumb and index,
like silk.
Conquerors, as Roman horsemen, around the ancient city's wall,
Lilar,
we are a single atmosphere,
a denouement now!
Ah, you are riding in through my nostrils!

NEW YORK TIMES WEATHER MAP

Weather Map, amidst this tiny print, you stand out
like a comfortable air of nudity. Amazing!
                    It's my air of nudity
in a stranger's bedroom
as my eyes alight on a most pleasing spot.

        LOW,
                    you're recorded right here,
yet during this same hour, 2000 miles away,
your vast spirit is
            HIGH
                    among the Smokies. You
show us in the 20th century of violence what a soul might be.

        Oh, obviously, concentrically, lovely,
your circles around a center of emptiness
have been watched by typists on vacation,
                    the mystically disposed, or me
—all the pebble-droppers at the still lakes!

            Look, look!
the bending, that contortion suddenly in those outmost circles,
            like an angel flailing to be free.
        I have been reading joyously the dear poets,
            and here you're mirroring their spirits
struggling to punch out of their lines and words
        to pin my shoulders to the floor.

        Weather Map, Oh, you who are inscrutable,
            I know you better than anybody.

What I would do if I possessed the signs that seem
to be music notes leaping and flying off the clef lines!
　　　I, as you, would dub them simply
　　　　　　　　—like "cloudy" or "clear."

VARIOUS PERFORMERS

The leaping of Maya Plisetskaya of the Bolshoi Ballet
in my life
and grace this moment of the slender dancing fingers
of my girl friend,
Daryl,
ripping the dry cleaner's plastic bag off her dress
—making a noise, *Swioshsh,*
that blows in like a wind

(like the illustrious west wind blowing over the ocean
and hewing out wave after wave of charioted horses
foaming at the mouth.
Sometimes my voice is swept up by this wind
and becomes one with this wind's wild virility.
O then I kick the covers off the bed and get up.

. . . from the ripping plastic loud is this *Swioshsh*
like the *buzzbuzzbuzz* overflowing the ears
of the terminal patient–narrator
in Emily Dickinson's poem, "I heard a fly buzz when I died,"
which I happened to be reading on Friday).

What did you say about the color of this dress, Daryl?
O leave it on the hanger and step out of your slip
gracefully

while the Earth is galloping like a circus horse.
Let's roll around or simply stand holding
nude as babies
as we ride

in eternity
like bareback acrobats,
concentrating,
let's ignore that distant *Swioshsh* I at times do hear.
A noise like the distracting applause of a crowd.

TO THE POET ON HIS
35TH BIRTHDAY ·

You think you are interesting and strong
if you resist making your wornbare shirtcollar symbol
of something or other. O this year
that goes by "like a cloud that changes and goes soft . . ."

Well, well,
one day you buy the mirror of your skittery intelligence lunch at
    Del Pezzos.
In a taxi after, she is riding closer to the far place of marriage.
She takes her young son your old companion—it's Whitney.
From the visitor's tower you watch the airplanes flying up from
    Kennedy Airport.
What a smooth takeoff Frank made by dying!

O my friends, good-by.
Goody-by!
My fancies,
Adieu!

Pretty things fluttering away one day
            you snatch at with a butterfly net.
        (At last, you have become a highly educated eccentric.)

Suddenly, it's February 19, 1967 tonight.
A halo surrounds Michael's head— His visual bliss is glowing
                        in the Mayfair burlesque

darkness, which welcomes Marianne and Michael and you
like three welcomed travelers.

Allan, look at Brandy's lovely leg!
She's dancing!
Now she takes off all her clothing because it is your birthday. . . .

AS IF

Whose is this? A rosy-sky color? Why it's your
                                        toothbrush.
Peering over the glass rim as if stretching with curiosity
                                        looking pretty
—it's so you. And in the mirror I see a very me grabbing it
and holding it as if I were a poster as if I held a flower.

Again the phantom curator
                        is frantic at this mirror.
                                The phantom
makes the tiled pleasant empty room appear as we disappear
behind the shower curtain as if
we go off to play among boys and women and giraffes,
their bodies spread brightly like nickels lost in the grass
                                (or hubcaps or quarters)!

                Welcome to my apartment.
Do you see me chained to this world like Shelley?
But often we are nude as the sun and also in the sky!

By the way, look—a slab of the universe comes to my window
                                like a Santa Claus.

Come over here. Maybe we'll recognize the sun
                as if it were me you saw for about the second time,
                as if it were you I saw for the first time.

VISIONS OF THE FUTURE

1

(you visit an historic village with your girl friend)

You get off the train and explore the streets of an old village.
The girl
you adore walks ahead to the museum of a holy church.
Her high heels
haunt you—over the cobblestones, clink, clink. Uncontrollably
you mutter Blake
to her: "Each village where you walk seems the haunt of holy feet."

2

(you visit a friend who has become a very rich man)

Look, a brightness among the trees! Gone! Was it Lucia,
the twins hand in
hand, or the gazelle?—delights brought here by your friend's
wealth and power.
In his perfect garden, you twinge with jealousy. Ah, another
brightness!
—Again it's gone away like a racing car that shone with
wealth and power.

3

(you teach European classics at the university)

You're quite a teacher exciting your students with a book
from another era,
Crime and Punishment. "Dostoevsky so skillfully makes Raskolnikov
live

in his special atmosphere," a student praises. They all are—
                              reading
about the old middle classes and the orgies of guilt—charmed
                              by another era.

        4
(you befriend a lost boy)

The features of the boy were puckered like a boy afraid
                              of a dark room.
Your hand's around his fanny, that's smooth as a pear,
                    as if you rubbed a pear,
                    if you felt like rubbing a pear.
What an admirable smile he has now. Look, like a light switched
                              on in a dark room.
Nowadays he moves, in the life of his friends, easily as a hand
                              fondling a pear.

        5
(you dine amongst strangers in the tedious suburbs)

The talk has been boring, but you take off your clothes with them
                              anyhow.
But they are not strangers when the friendship of nudity
                              is given breath.
Swift cries fill the air like honkings in a rush hour!
O how nicely you brush against each other like bumpers
                              in a rush hour!

        6
(you huddle with friends on a beach one cold autumn day)

The smoke of your breath rises into November.
                    The sea flips waves in.

The faces of friends, and smoke from their conversing merges
                                            with yours.
All the impulses of joy seem to merge like this visible breath
or like a kite and the tail, trapped in a crosswind and flipped about.

SONG OF BLOCK ISLAND (1)

You spot, as the Block Island–Providence ferry docks, a fire hatchet
  leaning
              forward like a flashy red woodpecker.
                    Or you might pass by
the waitress from Uncle Ray's motorcycling up to the bluffs with
  a young man
  from Penn State who will disappear from Block Island shortly.
Rowing the dinghy one morning, you recall pausing to love a girl
  named Edna
              on your way to Baltimore—
as you pull one oar, and Daryl, your lovely girl friend, dips in the
  other.

                    The evening hours,
many strong-limbed in Levi's step everywhere on the island toward
  music played
              in old Victorian hotels.
Feet, then more feet, give a presence as powerful as bluffs to the
  floor.
Feet, ready for action like the fire hatchet; and like it, they are also
  bare.
                  Most of all, bare!
Drinking beer on George's boat, you watch the southeast wind let
  fall
              its big load of fog upon the entire island
              without ever slowing down.

Of course, it does not surprise you that the ferry plodding from
  Providence to
              the decaying Victorian hotels

or that Daryl, her heels shoveling up sand as she runs the beach,
will out of the real world fall into
your dreams and come back up into
the real world, like
the dip of your oars,
in and out of the sea.

SONG OF BLOCK ISLAND (2)

Two tiger lilies on Walter's table, freshly cut.
You haven't seen Walter in years.
You'll come upon such flowers somewhere else.
But they'll be new tiger lilies.
When you meet Walter again, will he be new

like the tiger lilies?

Chilly. You duck your head under the sea.
Clearer than the Rockaways but not so crystal as Pago-Pago.
You see along the bottom a rock where
a crab scuttles. Then the sea, around your freestyle
and butterfly strokes, nods gently

as a tiger lily.

One has a raggy-doll wife, that one slams his fist.
These self-made ride in here on powerboats.
When in another bar the Musical Banshees play, the young shake
like flowers on a breezy day.
O they (never the hefty owners of the motorboats) are

like tiger lilies.

You need a toehold on the bluff to climb. You grab a
—yipes, it's poison ivy. Ugh! No, hurrah!
you're the boy of twenty-five years ago led to poison ivy
by idleness. Your eyes tear
in bright air. Standing in this vine now, you're

a tiger lily.

POEM

How many hours am
I a presence

        of grass?
Always windows
opened, & doors.
Populations found

        my kiss
                a new solar system.
O world, help! I'm so beautiful.
I caw-caw as though God
makes me
his parting gesture.
        "My old girl, Gretchen,"
I named

        a moon
one Xmas
because ears were being kissed the world
over. A Tokyo
factory worker revered his ear
like a new

        daughter.
O the newly-kissed in Genoa,
& my heart bulged like a mailbag.
I became 2 A.M. and part macaw!
Above a park
              (5 years after)

20

the footballs were booted.
              "Aya" up high!
     "Olé!"
a plump boy cried
a-waiting
one like love.
Yet, I was that night myself,

             my ordinary one.

A geranium was making

      the fire
escape pretty! "Dorothy,"
I shouted, "how could you say God
            is cold?
I sleep
     atop

     you
like your family roof in Hampton Bays."

THE HIGH RISER

The humanity of workmen on Clarkson Street is here!
One worker has awful skin; he drops his cross of cement,
                                        muttering.

But, Rainer Maria Rilke,
he has tried to live up to what you want him to.

                              What audacity!
Another, with the fine chin and dark curls of my grandmother,
resembles me. Were I a pretty fag,
on a steel girder we'd hold hands we'd sit so high above sea level.

The silver helmets are fishes who plop in and out of the ocean
as I look up the high riser.

                    WHOOO-EEEEE!
the lunch whistle whistles out my wild song, and the streams
of workmen toward me gently amble, O animals
                              of the Peaceable Kingdom.

I HAVE A FRENCH MIND

As the dust specks swim across my room, I decide to envy the
    Ape-man.
Tarzan danced the *dum-dum* with wild bull apes, and he nicknamed
    the sun
                  Kudu.
          Looking out of my window,
I count 10 kids leaving a school bus. I bite my lips!
I have the heart, the skin and eyes of Jesus walking by the tradesmen.
Only 15, Jesus poorly understood his love for the people.

After two minutes I'd leave the church of the Virgin de Guadaloupe
(famous churches are as boring as the Alps). But how, I wonder,
would Paul Valéry or Paul Verlaine view these cathedral windows?
"These 1000 religious heroes," they might write, "are big,
    ripe plums ready to burst!"
Suddenly, the famous church ceases to be boring.
I watch the old women, ambling to offer up prayers, as if they were
new facts.
Two candles, however, merely glow
until a memory of Max Jacob's prose
makes me think that:
Shedding wax tears, the skinny candle is acting, once again,
    like Feodor Dostoevsky. Ah, but the bigger flame
is the pure indifference of the Ugly Duckling to the bent backs
of the washerwomen, when he sees that he is truly beautiful.

Later, I go into the profuse marketplace, shopping.
"That fat plum," I say, "is ready to burst out of its skin
like myself NOW or like visionaries of medieval days."

Meanwhile, the Earth and I go round
and round, and
what I begin to think and feel today is like finding nickels
  in the snow!

At the Keneret Café,
I listen to my friend Peter, "When did the *New York Times* expose
how America kept Cuba piss-pot poor and agricultural?"
His words, the hour, this place—combine to be the rabbi of my
  infancy who, to cut my penis, holds me against my will.
But I do not really know this. I believe I sit here waiting
for a plate of cream cheese and raw onions.
If I were in my room, I might look out the window thinking:
"The goldfish swims below the purple sky of my neighbor's curtains.
A happy ocean! In this world only that goldfish is happy!"
Peter and I discuss America's immoral doings
in the rice paddies of Indochina.
But no more am I an ocean
heaving with moods of daylight and the coastal cities.
Why am I not in my tiny room? My sneakers with a rip 5 years old,
the house plant that grows taller like an only son,
and the radiator, quiet on warm days—
                    O what gentleness, what loneliness!
But I am helpless to go. The hands of the rabbi hold me here.
Those beautiful people who have caused me over the years
to sing and love or bruise my knuckles against the plaster—
they hardly seem to have
lived ever, as if I'd been circumcised only a minute ago.
"Allan," I say to myself,
"O Allan, now just the torture of the raw onion in your mouth
  will fill your life."

SHOWER

"Take a shower, Al, you should."

OK . . . feels good, the droplets
slapping me like a masseuse.
Well, there goes the sweat I got
in a hot corner
scribbling a few unsuccessful lines.
But that sweat was all I had left.
. . . Ugh! I'm clean
as polished marble,
on it my knowledge of
boys and girls doesn't adhere.
Hey, you Lilliputians
of H_2O
are stripping down my life.
But I'll let them
just so that when I will approach you
your legs rise
over the bed, spread,
our angel wings. . . .

HEY, COME BACK!

Welcome, beautiful day, into my window.
From behind an apartment house, the sun gives up its warmth
Like my wife sleeping behind the covers.

There's a bit of the sun!

Like my wife, or me or my young son
emerging from behind the covers. How did I allow someone
to borrow my family as if they're two books of poetry?
Hey, bring them back! They're not two books of poetry!
Oh-oh, the first time now—those long legs of my darling
are straddling the Earth like two pillars of Hercules.

THINKING OF FRANK

Maybe
ten years from now
down from my eye
suddenly one tear will come like a silver airplane
over the wide sky of the desert
but in Albuquerque
the new grass in the Alvarado Hotel
patio, before me here today, has the same bright green
as the grass where the minister who never knew you
had droned his nonsense about Robert Burns and you
and the traditions of poetry
three weeks ago,
where to drown his voice I'd shouted into my thoughts
"Frank O'Hara's collapsed from too much living.
O darling boy, get up, we love you!"

WIVES

My wife,
listen,
as my dreams waited for the various reds
of neon signs
there appeared instead a black clerk
walking from a municipal building's
curved iron gate
into the purgatory of traffic
bearing his hate for the whiteness of the supervisor,
until he comes to the gentle company of his wife's knees.
Some nights, in this chilly weather, as I remember you
made love to another man, I
know the anger of my hard-working Uncle Ralph discovering
BASTARD chalked on his tenement home; he
was reminded his wife's feelings about him
were mixed. Yet I would not have ceased
looking for the carnival of women whose kisses I felt
were French vowel sounds,
had I never come to rest by your knees
as if they were a log fence in the country!
MY WIFE, MY LOVER, MY REAL SISTER in the city
and only with you can I daydream of the church spires
of grass
in the right way.
I'm lying in the mud now.
My mother's divorce was once my lying in this mud!
I want to rest my head and say,
My white pillow and your hair are now ONE. Tell me, how
is the local weather
that falls from your breasts? At your knees

I and all my ancestors dream of making a pilgrimage.
Are your knees
signs?
And what will become of me here in the cold
mud? What shall cause the blood to burst through my head?
Grenades or a word?

AMERICA

Well, look, Allan. At the window
the light-hearted sun's napping like a house cat—also there's
    a frisky sparrow,
            and Secondhand Rose's successful antique store
        —it's the tip of America!
My, my, America, you do reach my window from California, three
    thousand miles
         without a strain in your muscles.
         Yet you always stay like a sweet kid!

(Allan, this old companion is at your window for you to whisper
    to her consolingly
         and softly.)
        "LOUDLY THE SAXOPHONES PLAY,
        TRUMPETS ARE POUNDING MY EARDRUMS!"
Listen, America, can you hear in this room my Ruth Etting recording
         of the parable of her fall?
         "Rats-from-the-harbor,"
just anyone who's ill-bred dances with her—for who can't afford a
    meager dime?
         "CUSTOMERS," she means, "TEAR MY GOWN!"
O America, I have sincere consoling soft words for Ruth Etting
and for the workers no longer young but who must dance nightly
    their role called,
         "Rats-from-the-harbor."

(Whoops! America, look at Ruth Etting's tenderness fill my dark
    eyes
         and go out into the atmosphere
            like fabulously successful Platonic love!)

Into the city Ruth Etting wandered from the open fields of Kansas,
        a sweet kid.
Exhausted in the peering footlights, while her heart is given to a
        gangster
            —What damage!
America, so free with your fabulous body and your more fabulous
        soul
            to bad men—Ruth is so like you!

But America, I thank you for giving the years I was your lover.
            Now I can feel,
as Hank Williams' western song is playing on my record machine,
my long, hairy legs stretching out into the vast, sunny Oklahoma sky.
            So I don't regret having known you, but
there is more parting us now than the burlap curtain on my window.
            Thank you, again.

Good-by— Say, remember Ohio at 6 A.M. waking up—the mist the
        grass and the cows,
                outside the window of our Greyhound bus,
                seemed like a dance concert.
And I'll not forget gazing down on the green of Iowa cornfields and
        the sunlit tops
                of tiny cars from Europe on the way
                to cowboys and to strange eating places!
O America, I could not have ridden these highways but with you
        hand in hand,
                stooping over the loony choreography of the pinballs.

But before you go, listen to this record. I'll turn up the volume. Wait,
            you'll find it full of pathos.
All my 35 years of living—from "goo-goo" to "oh fuck"—seems as if
        it has become
            the failing sight

of the old soldier lying alone on his iron bed in a lonely hotel room.
Can you hear? "O MOTHER GENTLY," he cries,
his eyelids closing, "ROCK MY BABY CRADLE!"
Look, off this hillbilly ballad the arm lifts in a gesture of finality!

HOMAGE TO ANDREW MARVELL

Poems about America's cruelties are our patriotic fervor.
I wonder how to articulate my disdain for America
with original fervor
as I rub your hand, keeping our love in its old habit of soaring
on wings "so strong, so equal, so soft,"
to use Marvell's words.
"You look as if I were a gorgeous peacock you just discovered
strutting through Central Park," you reply.
You think so? You *knew* me well— Once!
I am Andrew Marvell now and I'm shaking
all over in the utter strangeness
of my head turning my heart into a
5 alarm blaze, fed by the generous ideas of my era.
So what you might do, apropos of today, is get up and say to me,
"You never really think of me. This is good-by, *Andrew!*"
And I will wander into an Automat later, eat alone, then scribble
these words on a napkin: "Our love was begotten by despair
                    Upon Impossibility."

VOYAGE

The people on the wharf are waving handkerchiefs at you.
Wave good-by, Allan, and do not be frightened.
They're only your future, present—and your past!
Whoops, those people on the deck have grown smaller.
A fresh sea-breeze ruffles your collar tips like a pair of flags,
as forgetfulness shuts your eyes.
You're sailing toward the market busy in exchanging of hellos.
And as you come to foreign ways your curiosity
shall fly like the telephone wires over the continents.

PART TWO

SOUTH
AMERICAN
MUSIC

TO BUENOS AIRES VIA AEROLINEAS ARGENTINAS

The pilot is Latin; you wonder if he
has much mechanical aptitude.
Oh-oh, are the wings shaking from the blast of turbines, *naturally?*
You realize on taking off, "Hey, I'm not too young to die!"

While inching peacefully, the plane prudishly not tempted into
Sambas by Brazil or the exotic sun,
you listen to Rimski-Korsakov's Third Symphony
piped into a stethoscope, from Philharmonic Hall,
you've rented with strange pastel-colored bills.
Calmly, in your seat you fall back among the happy cellists.

The stewardesses distributing "pollo portuguesa" have round chins
that agitate you.
They are round like . . . something . . . all like . . . of course
. . . what . . . like
. . . no more wine, thanks . . . like
a heart attack suddenly insight strikes! "Yes, señorita, thank you!"
Their chins, round like their softly molded beautiful breasts!
Ah, Allan, only your metaphor discovers the trouble with the ladies
from Buenos Aires.

It's darkening, the sun drops. Only a thin red line lingers in the sky
as you have, Allan, at some parties—just hanging around
postponing the street
that shall reel in amusement over your foolish life, and
you put your arms around the silly; you make a friend.
"Just what is the shade of this red," you wonder. Anyhow, you sigh,
"Ah, flamingo red,"

half in tears pumped up from a newly discovered passion.
A passenger argues, if your young leftists would develop a tradition
as we have with our coup d'états, the 20th century would go by
                    without tear gas.
To an isle our president is flown, there are big flowers there.
First the general and his tank soldiers hear the alarm clocks go off
                    at 2 A.M.—
O the news of such good sportsmanship tugs you gently away.

On the earth, a hurt mother dreams somewhere her son is a doctor
to patients like these people in the air who sit in his office
with only the worries of the well-fed and the good,
where surely, you here, a stethoscope in your ears, are the idea of
                    another's emotions.
Look, waiting for the door to open, everyone is staring.
Now the travelers and you, at last, exist truly up in the air!

Oh, the being of such dreams. Invisible to the preoccupied of the
                    streets,
you cry,
as the lingering line of sunset is darkening.
Into Flamingo Red!

Many, many times in the years to come, you shall recall this trip.
"Ah, yes, flying," you will say. "Now that's real life."

IN BRAZIL

sipping an avocado cocktail,
I notice
two palm trees
growing out of the mountain top
up there
growing like two hairs
out of baldness, slanting forward
as a spondee marked on

"and no bírds síng."

                  Ah, avocado
and mountains and girls walking by
all become my familiars in minutes
at this fruit-juice counter,
where round shapes,
papayas and of names unpronounceable,
are piled highly—here in Rio where
appliances and I from America
seem always newly arrived,
the churning
of Dutch blood with Indian's (once in the jungle)
together thoroughly
with who can guess what other
(Of course, there are many Portuguese fathers).

By the pile of coconuts, the counterman's
electric Sunbeam Mixmaster whirls
—amuck-blood churning
(the same as wrought these strolling comelies)
of mangoes with fruit slices
of name unpronounceable
but sweet-smelling.
So full of vitamins,
the backs sloping swaying
of these girls strolling
by me, who leans prop-armed at the counter
and dizzy.

                         Hey, you, swarthy-skinned blondie,
perhaps it's your grandpa
who built the restaurant of Bavaria
that my book on South America
describes as,
"a bit of Vienna in the tropics."
Ah, it's practically
poetry, such guide's prose
conjuring for me: on the grass the garbage
and, smelling under a hot-penny sun, the bits of Wienerschnitzel
beside the weird pepper tree.

                    "on a cold híll síde."
As light falling between palm trees

into mind drops "on a cold híll síde,"

an old spón-dée,

and my zig-zagging racing flow slóws dówn.

40

Out of Brazil

train after train aboard another
of woody boards, Second Class
so completely,
a Quechua baby girl, maybe 3,
sucks, in Peru,
a milky-colored water
from Mama's tit,
these springs almost ruined by the past
little sucker.

                Later, this baby,
tucked under Quechua Mama's bench, fingers
two big meat bones. Beginning to whimper—
then baby Mama's toes, rough as the wooden slats,
bangs and bangs O wails
showing herself an awful indian kid.
Brandishing goo,
baby swings a Hershey wrapper
—O yowls, does she, as I'd do
if a nifty nuance were jostled out of my mouth.

                All the while,
Mama's been gazing into
the past or future
ahead stiffly like her nipple that's exposed.
Well, seeing her long nipple, one's mind dwells
on the finger of José Ferrer pointed at the jurors
in the *Emile Zola Story*.
      Those nipples, with grandeur of tallness.
           In this Dreyfus Affair, Gentlemen. I accuse you, Sirs!
         Terrific, wonderful

                    —No, not so! Look.
Mama's nipple is troubled with brown tiny bumps
as on an idiotic and beat-up face
of a boy hawking papers
I once had passed on a windy corner of Liverpool. . . .

SOUTH AMERICAN MUSIC

The most comfortable viewing of the ocean is from a restaurant
                                        constructed of glass
in Montevideo,
a monstrous PEPSI sign on the roof, which for miles
pinpoints this place of beautiful vista,
and in Argentina
you wrap around you a scarf of alpaca three handsome times.
Like the color of your eyes, it will be part of your personality
                                        the winters to come,
you foresee instantly in the store in Buenos Aires
that's exactly like a five-and-dime in Lima,
Ohio or Jacksonville
—All of which suddenly makes you wonder if you might walk into
                                        foreign twilight whistling
the plink of a Chopin polonaise dreaming of half-forgotten pagan
                                        gods like Melisande
as once quite good poets did well.

    Well, hardly! you think
watching my inamorata, Daryl, yank an elegant blue blouse
out of the elephantine bureau
then a gayer one with three colors
in the Gran Hispano Hotel.
Twilight Chopin, "Such corniness," you re-say
what you knew since you were twelve.
The smoke of a newly discovered *charuto do Brasil,* Dr. Pin,
                                        is dancing through your nostrils,
and you wait for Daryl's tall showgirly legs to go dancing
                                        into her stockings
flung across the sofa, heartlike

and closer to the time of Spanish colonial.
    "Like butterflies
my government thinks pacifists are harmless—so I'm safe."
In the vast-ceilinged, antique confiteria
your Argentine friend Miguel discusses the daring left-wing reporter
shot in front of the education building.
"Well, we have our own style of politics," he adds.
"When I was a young boy
to see soldiers by the school building was natural as the alphabet."
Like so many, Allan,
you have questioned the style
in your country of those who grew up breathing in the air of Camus
Kafka Karl Marx tough-minded Eliot and honest fearless Ezra
etcetera—
as when you pause for beauty under a PEPSI sign
rolling through the Americas.

Overdue now 3 weeks Daryl's period's uneasy amusement on the bus
through Uruguay's cattle country.
"U.S. dollars bought your soldier's underwear!"
as to a friend you spoke to Miguel, your politics boiling
like water.
Your words in your memory, after you leave Buenos Aires,
                              are an echo from New York,
one of the thousands of thoughts formed in the climate of Camus
Kafka Karl Marx tough-minded Eliot honest fearless Ezra etcetera.

    Up out of Porto Alegre up your ANDA omnibus
humming like anyone's early poetry queerly
in a vehicle alive with foreign humming
ela os tem abrigad ela
into a different air unevenly
away from the Brazilian port nervous
with sweat and pointless activity

like a good-by to the provincial family
and further away from where you are friendly,
                                        as city-hall politicians,
to be published across America.
And girls move in, as with you, as simply as water boils.
"It shouldn't slip, the diaphragm locks into the bones, right . . ."
Listen, Allan, "right, slip," leftover sounds of all of the others
who
are having discussions.
Oh, your life, Allan, out of the wintriness of Buenos Aires
is another Chevrolet
rolling into the middle of the mystery of
eucalyptus elephant-ear leaves in sunlit air
and spectacular views.

You dance on the waters of courtesy almost every day.
Needled by those delays.
You dislike the pulps thrown to the curb.
Oh poet Allan, like a creature from the American
        Junior Chamber of Commerce.

"The experience of living in Buenos Aires was powerful."
        Juicy brains fat shrimps
police dogs! god look their jaws are open
two bank clerks were John Barrymores!
"The experience of living in Buenos Aires was powerful
enough to stop the flowing of my precious blood for 3½ weeks,"
Daryl says, and you wonder,
"What's more like the workings of my thinking than Daryl's insides?"

—which is not to say a woman is a glimpse of a mystery.
"Funguses without names may develop there," Daryl adds,
                                "for no reason."
To say the sea is a great woman is as silly surely as

45

closing one's eyes dreaming in a Chopin polonaise.
On Gavea beach you know,
one day, Daryl is more the mystery
of eucalyptus elephant-ear leaves in sunlit air with spectacular views!

O sing praises of the diaphragm!
If a child grew certainly
affinities between your mind and her insides wouldn't teem so.
O sing!
"Sometimes my cunt itches for no reason," Daryl adds.
                              "It's a mystery."

Picnicking in Floresta Tijuca above Rio
when you find a man lying against a rock, unable to stop sobbing.
You begin to cry too. He is much older.
"How beautiful it all was," he says to you.
"Well . . . it was . . . oh, it was only a can-can dance.
Who couldn't learn to do it?"

POEM

I don't know whether I am light or heavy.
I'm light as a dollar
—No, so heavy,
I can believe it's me, not Reverend Edward Taylor,
who prayed
gazing cloudward,
"Oh Lord,
can this crumb of earth the Earth outweigh?
Love,
only the shining of the sun is simple today.
At the burlesque show
you said,
"The girls are so
agonizingly slow."
How do you, my dear, tolerate me
when I always wish the one lovely girl to be
dancing out of her fiesta dresses forever? . . .

MIND AND BODY

1

While propped on your elbows, darling, extending your chin,
you conjure Isadora Duncan
warming up to
perform; then comes a freshness of Elizabethan words
into her eyes.
They must have been as gems of Asia in her pure orbs locked.
On Monday, I read some lines by Auden
rhyming "curtain rod"
with "God."
A grotesque pairing!
No?
Yet pretty for being a bit grotesque
like the thighs of the female aerialist clutching the trapeze bar,
And flying!

2

My body at ease,
my eyelids close. A thought bounces
off a plank like the aerialist
as she can see the acrobatic camel and poodles and a nice ringmaster
rocking like a bell—
and this high one can hear joinings like "God" and "curtain rod,"
turning over, over—
rolling.
Down Isadora's cheek
a tear
that is (of course!) a pearl,
as the train chug-chugs out of the station

and Sergei, her lover, walks away then turns again to wave good-by
slowly.
Sergei, the poet, calmly notes, "the temperature of Moscow
drops in her absence."

3

Towards my body now yours eases in all that
inherited calm
of an Old World farmer when he drops the shovel to gaze
beyond the hayloft.
Thank you, darling,
for this. See me
in a quiet hamlet
as an obscure hoe-er
on the bed you've made
not at war with ancestors or self,
gazing—
Features, dearest, of the great world beyond the curtains
have been stirring my simple mind.

PART THREE

WATCHING PORNOGRAPHIC FILMS

PAPER AIRPLANE

Alexander Pushkin was part Negro.
So were the Wright brothers
who did a soft-shoe act up there.
Bad poets say, "this was Man
trying to reach the sun."
But to get to the point:
I lunge my adoration at you like a fighter jabbing
at the soft cartilage of the nose.
"Idiot," you cry, "look into your heart and write!"
OK. I'll try. How's this? Oh to lie
in the shade of Babylon's Hanging Gardens,
and ogle the best filthy pictures,
away from the eye of my boss, Nebuchadnezzar.
In addition, Love, when I am in a room with you,
my heart folds up
like a paper airplane
that flies out the window. . . .

THE DELIVERY BOY

When through the ancient screen door, the boy enters,
the daughter
shuts her Intermediate German grammar book.
She can recognize a delivery boy of the A&P
though she wears the thickest of hornrims.
He puts his bundle of groceries
down.
Hello.
        HELLO!
Supporting his arm, bottle-and-bag tired,
she guides him up into her sun-flooded nook
as if she were one of the old tarts of the Restoration
who, by a glee of sex and seducing alone,
lived.
To her feathery mattress
down, floating seemingly,
her legs extending
                    like an angel's wings.

ONE HOUR LATER

she bolts up from the bed. O
I gotta go to the john, Angel
Puss.
And hurries out the door.

MEANWHILE

surprised
Mother comes in.
O is my darling's beau a college boy?

54

He's so sensitive, she thinks,
he must be majoring in English!
Then as did her good looks, logic
lets go its grip on her. Mama
steps out of the stale flowers of her housedress
easily as a stortstop flowing into a play
area and Mama's nervous enthusiasm is so
the innocence of my teen-age dating,
her legs too have spread

out into archangel's wings,

as
her daughter strides back from the john,
O cooling Zephyrus,
as a breeze,
gently
the wings of these heavenly folk stirring!

THE PARTY

O I've never seen such a fine party. They
all are leaping fox-trotting or hullo-ing under
a showering of bright confetti. And balloons
now sailing in this wavering air. O and the gaiety
of tilted, dwarfish hats. O who can
have taught them so
many manners of fox-trotting? Plunk
in the center
of this room, hollow cheeks, by
horn tooting, blow
into a bubble. And way over
there, a masked boy
is regaling a mysterious chubby lady
who is also masked— Well,

and

ONE THING LEADS TO ANOTHER

And that is a new engine
of big thighs–bald spots–penises–curls–digits, digits
like the cotton candy
whirling
as at a circus, recalls the viewer.
Suddenly, but quite
predictably (if you ponder
the History of Man), one Man
disengages from the cloudiness of Society.

His eyes dazed with glory,
his legs erect over the masses

56

like one of the
wonders of the Pagan-wide world.
And half-opening his lips, O
will he sing of the body newest tunes
or simply of heroes?
Look, his testicles hang above us like ancient weapons!

HOME SWEET HOME

Mrs. Prudory is ironing folds out of her old
    simple print frock
        suffers a nose cold
            O dear where is my heatin' pad
                          when

                RING! RING!

! ! ! ! ! ? ? ? ? ? ! ! ! ! ! ? ? ? ? ? ! ! ! ! ! ? ? ? ? ? ! !
I say, you do owe this delivery boy a higher pay,
              O A&P!

THE GOOD PATIENT

OK! So he is a doctor.
Her heart's well-
being checking with his mouth
—No one has to tell me
or him either
he's chucking overboard
(the old heave-ho!)
the tenets of his good
friends and colleagues.
Slipping off her high-heel— My,
my, she's a charmer.

Day upon day
down looking up
every inch of such lovelies
wouldn't you
that white unsexy smock unzip
as he's doing now
and come out of those unstylish trousers
(a bit too pinstripe baggy)
and fling off that silly light on your forehead
and go to it right to it
like he's doing now
in his office? Of course
you would once
in a while— Wow! she's a sweetie
and

AFTER SOME TIME

well,
in that Some Time
on the examination table
they are
as vines
in a mid-Florida bog
become entangled.

O could this professional man and his good
lady disentangle
even if he chose to? And if so
would the lady, anyhow, consent
to lie by herself
as in the past
chilly and looked at?

This tangle they are
is as if I opened my *Gulf Road Map
of Kentucky and Neighboring States.*

(I believe it's still in my glove compartment.)

O my, but these roads have hair. . . .

TRUTH AND FALSEHOOD

Behold, you're in the sack with a great-looking lady! "I know from your eyes, you have been dreaming of screwing another girl all the while," she complains. Fooey! And you have this night just met her at a party. If it were my head she drew close to hers complaining thus—oo!

I would let her have it. "Miss, you are right. And a daughter of the Hapsburgs, that's who. So many afternoons, you see, on a horse has reduced to the utmost simplicity the pleasure in her of simply going up and going down—to say nothing of the spring it has put into her backbone!"

But perhaps, really, the fall of your bodies is interesting you. You might have said aloud (if she'd listen), "Feel, look at, our fingers quite cozily uniting. Yes, big decisions are always demanded in any part of the sky. So 20 birds have flocked all the way down here on our palms as fingers, darling."

Tomorrow or next November you may hunt for the immutable humanity of the other's inmost world, but the close society of fingers and toes will not again be as it is,

like a big tree passing you as you ride to, say, Pasadena on the Greyhound bus. An Olympian gladness! you sing, "Samson has just leapt past the window, his long hair flowing!"

While an old veteran barn-burner, sitting on the seat next to you, might at the same time be musing, "On one of the branches I saw a robin his head tucked in his gross body and brooding, no doubt, over his inability to put this tangle of leaves and branches in flames, like some barns he has seen from the sky—envious, as birds are, of the glories of those of us who trod the ground."

Fences, farmers, hills have jumped up as I've gone from one place to another in trains in a bus on a boat a bicycle. I observe Mother Nature constantly (that is anything going by), so I have learned to see myself. I've grown 3 inches shorter over the years due to straining my yawp to be barbaric,

but elegantly so of course like the blatant sun, and like sudden sunlight, a pleasure so that one may see clearer.

"Look, lots of publicity is what I want, Mr. Dickie Nixon, Hamphray or Johnston or whoever you are today. Of course, I'd be in a glass house throwin' boulders if I didn't own up to envyin' your whorlin' out a half-lie—whup!—quick as I can gulp a shot a White Lightning or Sneaky Pete— O excuse me, as I was saying,

"if you give me the proper publicity, I'll fix up the imbalance of America (since the payments sailed away for Europe and Asia) with a string of longish poems, although this strain on my body will shrink my height some more inches, maybe 3 to 6. And I'll be a martyr

"which, like dreaming of soaring flight, is heavy going, a headache! But, at this hour in my life, to become a midget! I accept the ultimate challenge."

The ultimate challenge, I said. O my mind has never been so gorgeously free! Someone, gag me! No, listen! Stop me! To my lips the biggest whopper of my life is rising. Attention:

        I'm Allan Kaplan
        5 feet 11½ inches
        slightly   balding
        and when I write
poetry, the smoke of a mild cigar is often drifting through my
nostrils. . . .

PART FOUR

AVE MARIA

MARVELOUS

Ah my Jill loves her nakedness
and rock 'n' roll
like a fox loves hidden places.
And Marina's teats
are my darkest lilies
(she thinks she has a colored grandpa).
O Dorothy whom I no longer know is made long
like Palestine,
I'm a Wandering Jew.
And Tania flings shoes off, fresh
as a comet in the sky.
And Tania's over forty!

ARS POETICA

Leroi Cooper, driving up to your river-view house
in your shining Impala Chevrolet
you might possibly dream of yourself following in
the tradition of, say,
Percy Bysshe Shelley,
the *Pearl* poet, Samson
Agonistes, Alfred
Tennyson or Dante Alighieri
to cite but a few
who have lumbered along a similar path
which, Leroi Cooper, best-friend of my youth,
when down you step into the grimy New London Railroad
Station,
you start on.

I can imagine you, day after day,
seeing out of your car window
the sprawl of moderate-income housing
which brings into mind high school
girls you used to date
resignedly,
who took ballet classes
although their bodies had unclear
shapes as these moderate-income housing projects
past which, Leroi, you must drive
before you can from the white-columned
colonial porch,
like a great poet
who has strained up,
gaze down serenely from your private mountain perch

at the Navy's submarines
into Connecticut's Thames River
submerging
like fat beasties down into an older river.

Leroi, if you ever wonder about me,
say, how I am with the commonplace
of those
entering, becoming friends, a few going
on like you;
while your Impala drives you up to your palace,
inhale a pasture's clover mingling
with cowslip and cowdung
by the highway,
an odor self-contained
and contented,
as if saying "Screw you,
Screw you," to the cars rolling by.
Leroi, if you ever wonder about me,
say, how I am with the commonplace
of those
entering, becoming friends, a few going
on like you;
while a cool breeze blows across your white-columned porch,
gaze at all the arms waving on the fir trees.
At the river
these trees are whistling,
O they whistle up to the speeding moon, like
a well-bred maniac.

During my graduate studies in English literature,
I perspired
all over Despair
like a detective shadowing spirits like Dante up to

the only
hilltop of Affirming
located just above Resignation.
But, Leroi, you and I might call "Hey, why all this?"
because the pleasure
of poetry was actually born
one day
on your lawn
under the spray of your water sprinkler.
A girl, Mimi, directed her half of the bed into
the moving truck.
They have run from me, sometimes,
like roaches from a hasty shoe.
And a crazy taxi cab ran down an old friend, Hank;
since the time on your lawn.
"O they flee me," I have read,
"who sometimes did me seek."

Leroi, we were half-drugged by telephone poles
speeding by
as we sat in your Uncle Ralph's auto. Remember,
mountains and Montana
made us lively.
Behind a tree trunk, giggling
we peed long streams,
imitating, but privately intimidated by,
Old Faithful geyser
shooting into the sky,
and your Uncle Ralph, who had a bad prostate,
said enviously of Old Faithful's hourly regularity,
"Only Nature could have such a good bladder."
From Hong Kong from Czechoslovakia
from Ukrainia and Baden-Baden
across continents and oceans

70

the fire of colored postage stamps burned in our hands.
The one you showed me from Madagascar,
it was wide and a watery blue-green
like the eye
unseen and approving all of your soap-sculpturing,
your match-book covers and your mimicking.

Day after day, Leroi, you drive up from the station.
While your wife prepares,
your connecting to the river-life
from your white-columned porch
is always living by a truth one has found
to live by always.
Is this you! Listen to this, Leroi Cooper:
to be born under the lawn sprinkler's
cooling spray,
to grow up emulating the ocean
of climate over the Earth
every minute,
like a cart rolling
—scorching winds, chilly silences—
one rolling atmosphere
of Affirmation, Resignation, Giving-up, Affirming.
Ah, three rubber balls orbiting in front of the juggler.

POEM

Down the stoop, 2 screaming boys ran to fill their hands with a rubber ball. Wow! That's typical of 3rd street.

"I brushed against Nina on the Vera Cruz beach!" my painter friend, Dominick, said.

As I've never come miles near to the face of this Beautiful Girl and Dom's green, docile sea, I can only too vaguely remember myself rubbing the sand off her shoulders. And I began to feel, turning the corner, empty as the hands of a schoolgirl as she daydreams of a husband.

"Dom, did you ever notice, when people sit around a statue, a hand reaching up to rub the toes?"

"Once I touched a bronze toe, and a museum guard grabbed my hand. I was 8."

Meanwhile, uptown, brilliantly mirroring the sunlight, the highest windows resembled window gardens—a petunia, a cornflower, a rose, all in a line, just like little boys in Hitler's Youth Corps.

"Still, while we're here, a toe somewhere is getting shinier," I said.

Walking into a draughty courtyard leading to Dom's studio, a set of dark working pants and a green towel, above us, and a rose-sky blouse lurched then sidled like a rose or a cornflower in a window box as if they were those high windows themselves, rising up against a rule of their lines, rushing to mix at the horse races. Ah, this leaping in our world eternal for the first thrills of the big city and a $2 window.

"What smoother sex could an 8-year-old kid have than rubbing the toe of a Rodin? Yow!" I cried.

Of course, presently I recognized the rose-sky of the blouse, the greenness of that towel to be the ghost of Arshile Gorki. How could I claim the appearance of Arshile a total surprise? No, not since Dom discovers the glow, outside his window, is the sun revealing its identity, like the bragging of a master spy. Years ago, in a concrete parochial schoolyard Dominick had sat heartsore; a beauty of orange olives was eclipsed by the whiteness of the long nuns. But that was St. Louis 20 years ago.

"Ah, Arshile," I thought to myself, leaning out the window, "this burning of 5 o'clock sun is the orange ball flying in the middle of Nothing."

MY WIFE'S TONGUE

Listen, don't open up my wife's tongue.
Old oil landscapes are stored inside—
of cows and dozing sheep. I've known
some that made me say:
"Last night, O a tongue better than
money in the bank!" Or, "That tongue is
sweeter,
in an odder way, than cantaloupe." But
that of my wife
is like a fawn. It keeps a good
humor of waves by tugboats on the East River. Yes, happily,
my wife's tongue, in the morning,
is without mystery.

My friend,
I can tell something from the strong look of your eyes.
"Oh for a tongue that is like the pierced host,"
is what you
desire on your wedding night—or is it a tongue that's
a lamb
caught in the tiger's teeth? Take
my advice,
an ideal tongue is a doll
opening and closing its mouth. Write this 150 times
as though it were a prayer, and you will
meet a tongue as
dazzling as a parasol.

And
I knew a tongue years ago

that was the roll of a river,
the dream of sidewalks on a summer's day;
arriving like a "Hallelujah"
of a big peasant after
Lenin got off the train. I thought,
"This arrival will be the kingpin of reminiscences,
dearer than the memories of my army buddies."
However, soon
my wife's tongue rode into my mouth,
an invasion
of the tulips
too lonesome to stay
inside my old 6th-grade geography text.

LONG ISLAND

My bare feet are like 2 old friends among these trees.
Lounging on Earth with no plans,
the wild roses are the summer of Guillaume Apollinaire.
"Inside you, dear Allan, a taste," Guillaume writes,
"of ripe beach plum stretches like the chest of the deer."
Apollinaire writes here as if he were near as my bare feet are near!
Caw-a-caw, above these wild roses lounging on Earth,
a seagull sings as if it were not in the 20th century.
And onto the Earth the sun-glow falls like a great Greek wrestler.
And today you, Walt Whitman, surge through our air like telephone
    wires.
"Al, O, Al Kaplan!" I christen a deer I know roams these woods,

                  that I have not yet seen. . . .

TONIGHT

Looking up while scratching my kneecap, I saw you, young star.
    What luck!
I am so partial to whatever glows
    as a lighthouse or as myself
    who am a fire fed by

Claire Dom June Dorothy Michael Kathy Rici Whitney Gunther—
    what timbers! I add more lovers and friends.   Look,
        I burn more extravagantly tonight.

                                Listen,
good luck to you out in the heart of the universe, burning.
                                  I must confess
                                  my burning
extravagantly in this land of ideals and slaughter is impossible.

                My friendship
for you is a sudden storm where there arises a vision of the young
meteorites about you being everywhere snuffed out
                in the frigid darkness.
                Good lord, are we cousins?

        I must go,
                although I remember
now Walt Whitman's embracing of the universe and you tightly,
                            with my neck strained upward.
How nice if I remained and my mind then unlocked a thousand
    doors to you,

but my new girl friend is wringing her hands waiting. Smack
                              in my opened hand, hers
                              will be, to
the "screw you" of living, wild star, the ultimate guiding star
                              and opposing phenomenon.

THE RED BADGE

After the cinema's air-cooling, onto steamy pavements.
Summer toyed with my crotch with her sweaty touch.
Yet I looked around as if I were looking for a regiment.

I felt at home at the jib of the 25-foot sloop—
the sea, with a diplomat's bowing, falling rising falling.
Yet I felt a pang at being separated from the regiment.

The coolness of the forest was busy upon my skin,
under the towering of the graceful pine trees.
There I heard, for a second, the sound of my lost regiment.

The soldiers care for each other and sing together
because of the wounds.

JULY POEM

The sun beats down as if it were in a frenzy over broken promises. The heat of the concrete and walls seems as if it would begin to howl like Sioux with rifles sold by the bad white men. You drop into your chair like a good man who is deciding what to do next. The Atlantic Ocean, the Pacific drift by your mind's eye. O daydreams!

Presently, a plain-looking robin attracts you with its twittering on the fire escape. These robins, you note, are no more unusual than working girls. But how peculiar and lovely—your heart, nevertheless, is banging wildly. You sing, you get up, as if your passion wasn't totally hopeless:

> O do not, dear, warble by windows any more,
> Your song shall the concert halls ring-O
> if you tonight my world-weary finger cure,
> if you let it lie under your soft wing-O.

You fall onto the couch, the bird flies away as if to a cloud. You try to prop up on your elbows, but flump! like a fighter who cannot rise, you collapse. You lie there as if to get up would mean that the blonde sweetheart would be shot by dark gamblers. "So once," you say, "I was a sweet-faced, gangly prodigy carrying a violin to class. So now here is the end of all integrity and of the road to my championship fight." And your eyes begin to close like curtains.

"Yet," you add, "how sweet it is to be knocked out cold. . . ."

MY STRANGENESS

I glide
forward, and then like paperclips from a rubberband
                    I am flung
                        with adamantine fury
to the end of this line of poetry here
where the love poetry of four hundred years is burning.
        And whoosh! One more leap!
Later, I rush down the stairs.
The wild motions of history impel me into an ever-hurtling subway,
            out at 34th Street.
                Forward, always!
                    O whence cometh my joy?
The sunburn of my skin, the wonder of my eye, and the beasts
grazing on my 20th-century brain
                    blending into a tall frame that's me
like the 50th and 51st floors of the Empire State Building
—which I look up at
now with four centuries of love lyrics alive like roses inside me.
The steel on its top, I notice, and the windows are glowing
            like flowers
                similarly!
Like Tristan, I gaze as though she were Isolde. My goodness,
she's straightening herself up a few inches to delight me!
            Knowledge is born in me once more like
another season: This new perversity is a big sea-turtle
            in a clyme balmy
                far away,
            But close-by
the sunlight greets midtown and me with the warmth of a seasoned
        traveler

who's gone native
                    suddenly.
Through new streets I go like my life, aimlessly. I stop to greet
the sun's new personality, which is for here more florid than is usual,
                    but I'm hurried on, no
                    I slow up,
                           far away is nearby!
The animal of my perversity stirs on stumpy legs, and the sand falls—
        Ah, I can feel its hard back so warmly thumped!
                    across my brain
                    surprisingly.
I go into a new street again, as the waves come gracefully,
            with grace always.
Now the sea-turtle is slapped by the warm fingers of the great ocean.

THE HEART

My baldness is a tragic but a beautiful disease,
    I noticed by the mirror, today.
    "Now I want to hear a wondrous idea,
    which figures in your discourse, daily,"
I say, distant from my life, as if I'd become one of the poets
lured from his writing table by the ignorance of a dark Arab boy,
as I hold a dialogue with whoever the ancient poets called the heart.

ALMOST CHRISTMAS, 1969

On Sheridan Square nothing unusual
is going on. Off the Square, the Church of St. John is
here all grey and as always the Snow White letters
(forming a pious thought on an opaque bulletin board)
seem frightened; but
5 years walking toward your home past here,
the *R*'s, the *L*'s are always
seemingly terrified of their own fair beauty—
so absolutely white, the *B*'s *W*'s those *T*'s
etcetera
etcetera. And still no cold invigorating
and today it's Christmas nearly
and no snow whorling, O lovely
down
. . . nothing better to do but go home, turn on
a flick that the TV section of this N.Y. *Post*
(under your arm) has informed you of
called, "We've Never Been Licked." Well, well! The
reviewer says it's "a romance of college days."—
Ah no, you just know this picture won't be as interesting as it
sounds.

But just suppose
you began to flee up the Church of St. John's steps,
at your back, gangsters shooting or editors or anyone
hating the poems
—then Sheridan Square, today, would be a touch
that feels more interesting,
eh? Bang

84

BANG

And as the whistling meteorite falling (of lead also)
through black seas of space by accident strikes a
heavenly body, so likewise
the whistling shot
now and then is stopped
in its going; a sooty crater rose
on your back
as on a moon. However, you, you're upright
still, but as if you just mastered the trick of walking,
zig-zagging,
you drop— Well
hi-de-ho! The Square is a touch less usual.
O how then could snow
hide-in-cloud
and not fall feathery all over
you, as over James Cagney
in front of the church door sprawled likewise
in *The Roaring Twenties?*

And in James Cagney's closing eyes,
did the street grow still whiter
and exaggerate itself foolishly like thighs
inside the thoughts of
a 15-year-old boy who's bashful who's not thus far been fucked
by anybody?

. . . but on the steps of the Church of St. John,
as if Miss Snow White, pink-faced the Intimation
of your Sex-Life-Future,
kneels by your sprawled body, before dancing
off to the dwarf's cottage, there endless
pleasures. O laughing and hairiness!

O Man, you're awful horny ooo!
sad adieu!
Today's message on the bulletin board you can still read:

CHRIST

MAY NOT HAVE

YOUR ANSWER

BUT COME ON

IN HE MAY JUST DO

THE TRICK

IMMEDIATELY

"THE TRICK"?

BEFORE EASTER POEM

England under Queen Anne
grew wealthier than ever,
my history says.
Under Queen Anne— And prospering!
O good Jesus,
under your cross
you grew poorer than ever before.
Yes,
I've felt closer to English literature
than to you, most of the time;
but, good father, this day
I can appreciate your rough going.
I'm a little overtired too
and feel a few splinters in my back.

THOUGHTS OF A
VICTORIAN GENTLEMAN

I contemplate settling a warm island.
I feel England's cold
climate in the eyes of the poor.
Bright greenery, somewhere, spits out pineapples of gold.

But I suppose I tend to, and am tended by, too much
too much, our domestic girls.
The apple-tint blushing
upon one fair-one's cheek does cheer me.

Although I'm proud as a pineapple,
I foresee the end.
But I've felt in my hot breath,
a spirit so grand
it dwarfs the colossal dinosaurs
flying in ancient eras.

We should act. Doing, doing more is to wake
from my limp thoughts
of lagoons
where brown women swim
out shaking themselves on shore
naked
glowing
as the bright buttons

on a factory owner— Oh damn this new class all!
From their dim buildings

the waifs are thinning
trickling **out**
not eating.
Listen, one waif heaves a gurgling sigh
of a freshet splashing a woody countryside.

                                   Outside
becoming one—like my glass pieces glued,
afire above the fireside on my mantel—
Alf and Nellie
are braving the cold, clinging.

Calamities are crashing
into the lives of our poor like the colossal icebergs
upon the lovely shy heiress of our stories.
In the water's churning, her silks turn to heavy anchors!
The poverty-stricken everywhere are being crushed.
O calamities thunder like
ice slabs breaking off from the polar cap of the spirit.

                                 O listen, listen,
                                    the euphony of reform.
Do you hear it chiming on the ear's nerves and flesh?
I will slip from my selfishness
easily as if from my waistcoat.
I shall plunge,
as the hero of the charming wandering picaresque novels of my youth,
straight down to the maniacal river of our uncertain times.

"You are safe," we say to the lady, "touch the strand.
You are soft as a flower.
Look! ahead a dawn brightens the darkness of the sewing
machines.
O my lady, you have the color of milkiness and apples.

Let my arms dry you like the sunshine.
Ah, you are a flower,
a species of the light lily in my January
of cold and fog and coughing."

AVE MARIA

Mary, so full of calmness
—Hello.
With you, this place up to its high vault is familiar as my pillow.
This is a Palace of Rest,
and all my freakishness has become a memory like yesterday.
And how sweetly you're staring down as if roses grew on the floor!

Here, catch this flower;
this is a place for Civility.
You are, I tell you, with always young eyes and despite your many
years,
like no one else.

By the way, Mary,
I saw your son on a high-school track today.
His nearly hairless, white, muscular legs were keeping him ahead of
his disciples. . . .

THE USHER

Nice! Stars lie in a friendly town. Moon,
you have the air of somebody
I once knew. Whoever you may be,
tomorrow come to the matinee. Children will see
a duck laughing above the barnyard as a test pilot,
daffy
and famous as Dali is. Their giggles will
be my memory of Garbo's
eyes
making the baron's jewels shine. Moon,
my hobby is
good memories.
This is the
century when the nephews of German brewers,
in a rage,
had no respect
for almonds
in the eyes of Jewish schoolgirls.
I knew the hypocrisy hidden in
Shirley Temple's smile
would bring no good
to Germany. . . . Moon, why you are Hank, the cowpoke!

When last I saw you, you
were a cowpoke
riding out of Silvertown
with the dust rising above your spurs.
I thought you'd get asthma!
After these years you have come back

to help the ladies who had hopeless
love
affairs since leaving boarding school.
The glow of yourself
walking in the sky
makes them feel the spirit of Clark Gable
carrying logs to a fireplace.

Well, Hank, you have finally
made it
big, riding above the desert. Yesterday,
on the movie screen, a young man
held up a filling station, bitter
about his sister being forced into a house
of ill-repute, and cried,
"O poverty has made me bad!"
He did a portrayal of Christ rising.
He rose from the grave of poverty
to become president of an airplane factory.

Was the Lamb's ascension
your example, Hank, to rise into the sky?
The Lamb
is the spirit of
our city's beauty—including
the girls hidden from
us
behind shower curtains
as they wash
their long hair.

Sit there on that chimney
a while. Dear Hank,
you are the only white man

the Apache could trust. Hear me.
I, after the midnight show, opened the door!
Hundreds of eyes came out and
stared at the traffic signals, they crossed
an avenue like
"big boys"
going to a matinee.
So I, in my white gloves, had been the Holy
Ghost

although
those eyes want to rest
under the warm covers
of Clark Gable's eyelids while Clark
is kissed by the lady
newspaper columnist,
at this moment
while you are tiptoeing along the roof's
rim.
Hey, don't fall
off!
I know
you're behaving like a stunt man
just to make Honeybelle smile. She must
dance all night
in the saloon. Her legs are hurting, and
the smoke is making her cough
blood.

DRIZZLING

It's drizzling upon my heart
and drizzling into the streets
outside, so why can't I simply sing
out words as Verlaine sang,
"Il pleure dans mon coeur/Comme il
pleut sur la ville."
Water is boiling, hie thee to the oven
but you open up *Lunch Poems* instead.
Along easy
goes the River O'Hara like a spilt martini
leaving all as the poised upright stately glass
helpless motionless.
O try, Allan—if I were only *fou*
like Verlaine, winsomely. But to coo
in quaint hotels at Rimbaud
embarrasses you.
You feel silly, merely a thought embarrasses you.
About your girl friend's dancing job arrives in her letter
from Las Vegas
today and the normalcy of your suspicions embarrasses you
further. . . . Allan, say, who is
entering here? . . . It's your Muse
whom you don't know nor cannot see,
she laughs at you now
as you choose what word you adore more
"iffy" or "Medea."

HUDSON STREET

The buzzing of passing diesel trucks steadily buzzes near
as my own fingers are.
And as I cross my eyes as I used to in P.S. 3,
the fireproof, 6-story warehouse jumps off the corner.
"Love yourself or whoever today" (I listen)
"with the confidence of your new polka-dot necktie."
This is the horn of the ocean liner I hear
booming my horoscope out
for today, June 22, 1965!
O this day is drunk as the mad father of the Karamazovs,
and I am its marvelous boy.

SANTA FE

1

You see, one festival day, the persons of your own imagination,
   half-naked
            darkly, men of long yellowy feathers.
            They bow to the grass
         for only a dollar.

            Bells, bowing and bells!
               In between similar great instances
         (as when you
            met a lovely sandy-haired lady, or a fanatic hummingbird,
or the tree on Calle Otero that bends to a wall like a wailing woman)

you still feel you are a bird with wounded wing.

2

Her warm neck on your fingers becomes the warming word "I"
   which fills your poems.
               ". . . don't know, really,
if I'm frightened or happy at feeling disengaged from house and
   husband,"
         the sandy-haired lady confides to you
               as if you were known
                  like the gold around her finger.
                     So naturally!
Then northwards she
            goes, oh broken-winged bird in Santa Fe.
         And you are, Allan,
         alone even more

until two lovely people, Hillary and Charmaine Crown,
open their big house where they feed you.
Then on a gentle horse they mount you.
And, oh, you ride!

WELCOME

Only you delight touching that fuzz in my ears.
When I know your gestures are mysteriously formed somehow
by hollyhocks you watched in California from your window,
I might deeply think of the minds of Conrad or Proust
—I can think logically about *their* emotions at least.

But hail and welcome! I'm brightly focused on you today. Hello.
You are in my house simply and eagerly
like the music from my radio by Brahms,
which the announcer afterwards assured me is really Mendelssohn's.
We kiss!

The personality we make together, we welcome once more.
Your husband and I, you say, are both Jewish;
you clap your hands. We Jews are a part of your fetish, I reply,
and we kiss again. And what's there to say of the days
we hurry to each other,
our bodies hurrying to keep up with us?

71 72 73 10 9 8 7 6 5 4 3 2 1